writing essays

. . .

janet godwin

Blackwell's/Palgrave Study Guides

Pocket Study Skills

For a complete listing of all **Palgrave Study Skills** titles, please visit:
www.palgrave.com/studyskills

contents

Introduction

Essay writing is a skill needed at college or university whether for coursework or exams. This booklet aims to give students quick fix tips to get them underway with essay writing and max out their marks with handy tips about what tutors are really looking for.

Many of the tips in this guide are developed in the *Palgrave Study Skills* and *Pocket Study Skills* series, so these may be your next step for more detailed advice. Specific links are suggested at the bottom of the page throughout this guide.

See *Planning your essay* Ch 4.

analysing and planning the task

1 Dealing with the question

Your essay title has lots of clues in it. It usually has an instruction word – which tells you what process you have to go through, lets you know the subject under study and suggests any limits to the question.

Instruction or process word
- Critically analyse …
- Outline …
- Describe …
- Justify …

This will tell you the depth you should go into – *critically analyse* is to go into great depth, so you can probably only cover a small research area. But *outline* means show you know the key areas to cover.

Subject or content – this is your focus. Think carefully before going outside this, however interesting it is. For instance, if you are asked the history of the subject, stick to a few lines only unless specifically asked to cover it.

Limits or scope of the question – look for any *limits* in the question such as **contrast two countries** or **give examples from the last 10 years.** Stick to these absolutely.

Other aspects – anything else in the question after you have identified all the above.

2 Dealing with the assessment criteria

Step 1 – find the criteria

Make sure you have your assessment criteria to hand. These may be in a course handbook, handout or buried in a virtual learning environment. They are worth seeking out as, much like a job interview, the closer you can match the job specification the better your chance of success.

The criteria are likely to be divided into *assessment* or *marking criteria* and *learning outcomes.* The **learning outcomes** are what you are expected to demonstrate you know in your work and the **assessment criteria** are how these will be judged and usually include academic criteria such as critical analysis, academic style and referencing correctly. This is the best clue you have to what is in your tutor's head.

Step 2 – gather any other information you have been given

This may be a suggested structure, guidance notes, resources you are expected to draw on, reading list, a marking feedback sheet – useful, as it usually has the assessment criteria on it in a simple format and with any additional information such as a case study or a model sample assignment.

Don't ignore this stuff. The tutor spent time putting it all together and expects you to use it – it will gain you valuable extra marks.

Step 3 – analyse all the above

Now the clever bit – and if you do this well you will not only save time, you will boost your marks.

Lay out all the material in front of you – if it is all in a virtual learning environment then copy and paste into a Word document and print it out. Take time to work out how the title links to the learning

See *Planning your essay* Ch 1.

outcomes and assessment criteria. Try to see where the links are, what exactly will gain you those marks. Scribble this down. You may notice that it is not the content alone which gets you marks but usually your own analysis that comes from what you read. Get any first thoughts you have down. This is the start of your essay.

Planning

Time: You will need to roughly plan your time and your essay outline. Find out your deadline and work backwards from hand-in until now.

Here is an example of a time and task line for an essay set on 1st November, and due on 27th November.

Time	Task	Completed
lst-4th Nov	Groundwork Things you need to know Word/page count division Do task timeline Analyse question	3rd Nov
2nd-7th Nov	Preliminary research	8th Nov
7th Nov	Plan	9th Nov
7th-10th Nov	Research	12th Nov
10th-14th Nov	Write draft 1	15th Nov
14th-16th Nov	Revise plan/edit	16th Nov
16th-18th Nov	Further research	19th Nov
18th-20th Nov	Write draft 2	16th-21st Nov
20th Nov	Revise plan/edit	22nd Nov
20th-23rd Nov	Further research and draft 3 if needed	-
23rd-26th Nov	Edit	24th Nov
26th Nov	Proofread	25th Nov
26th Nov	Checking	26th Nov
27th Nov	Hand in	27th Nov

(Work backwards)

Targeted reading/researching should be carried out before and between drafts

See *Planning your essay* Chs 2 and 3.

If you have several essays/assignments, it may help to do a planning grid or use a wall planner for the stages.

Date	Essay 1	Essay 2	Presentation

Planning tools: These are entirely up to you so choose what works for you.

Consider these:
- mind-mapping
- linear lists with bullet points
- jotting random thoughts anyhow
- individual ideas on sticky notes
- PowerPoint slides
- table or matrix

The most important thing is that you get your initial ideas down. Check these against any assessment criteria, learning outcomes and other information you have gathered and add or delete anything you cannot see fits in. At this point it is worth doing some quick research to find out which areas you can find reading matter on. A lack of this means you may have to change the focus of your essay since no research evidence to support or refute the subject means no academic discussion – so few marks.

You may also consider reducing the area(s) under discussion (you can make this clear in the introduction) so that you can be more analytical – do check you can still meet the assessment criteria, though. What is left after this process is a basic essay framework for you to fill out. The next step is to plan your basic structure so that you limit the research you do to fit your word count.

structure – what goes where?

Starting with your word count (yes really), divide up your essay into sections. Just knock the end nought off your word count to find out what 10% is.

For a 2000 word essay:

- 10% for your introduction = 200 words
- 80% for the middle = 1600 words
- 10% for the conclusion = 200 words.

This is important to note as this is your budget. If you over-research and overwrite you will end up doing three times the work you need to. Much better to notice how much you can write for each section now, so you can attempt to stick to it.

Organising the middle

A paragraph will probably be around 200 words, so calculate roughly how many paragraphs that will be. In this case about 8.

Look again at your learning outcomes and assessment criteria and identity the main areas you *must* cover. Allocate one point to one paragraph. If you can, put them in order but don't worry too much if you can't. That will come to you later.

See *Planning your essay* Ch 5.

3 What goes in the introduction

A common problem is that your introduction becomes the essay. The introduction is only an introduction to THIS essay, not the whole subject. Try writing it last so that it reflects what you actually did.

What an introduction needs to do:

- Tell your reader why this is an important area to study.
- Give the reader a guideline so they know what you are going to do and how you intend to tackle this. You may have to justify this. If you need to limit the areas you cover in order to do more critical analysis, this is the place to do it.
- You **may** tell the reader what your position is or what you intend to argue. This is usually optional although some subjects (history, politics) prefer this.

4 What goes in the conclusion

The conclusion is your last chance to impress. Often students' conclusions do not match the quality of their essay and research. So be clear here. Your reader wants you to pull it all together for them and point out clearly what you actually found out, **your conclusion** based on **your findings** and maybe any **implications** of your conclusions. Your reader does NOT want to trawl back through your work to try and figure out your conclusion for themself. Making it easy here for the reader is the way to good marks so do leave yourself time to do a good conclusion. It will pay off.

What a conclusion needs to do:

- Clearly state what you found out.
- Draw a conclusion from these findings.
- Indicate any implications of your research for your own practice, the profession or even any policy

---

See *Planning your essay* Ch 6.

changes that are needed. You may suggest future actions or research, but keep this brief as this is only to indicate you know that your essay is not the end of the matter.

No new information should be introduced in the first part of the conclusion (the first two bullet points). The most common mistake in student conclusions is to come to a conclusion that is not there, that you did not provide evidence for in your essay. So check that anything you mention in this part of the conclusion really IS addressed in your essay. If it isn't, **take it out** (or put it in the essay and evidence it). Be harsh with yourself here.

5 Writing up the middle

Don't forget to keep an eye on what goes in an introduction and conclusion, but for now concentrate on the middle. You need to produce coherent paragraphs, signpost your reader through these and use academic style and referencing.

What a paragraph needs to do:
- Each paragraph should develop one point only, which should be clear from the first sentence or two.
- Provide supporting evidence from a variety of sources for (and maybe against) this point.
- Consider if you need to link this to your own experience/practice or examples of practice in your field. This illustrates you can link the theory you have learnt to practice.
- Come to a mini conclusion. From the evidence you presented decide what you think but avoid using 'I':
  - *the evidence here suggests …*
  - *this shows/indicates that …*
  - *so …*
- Link to the next paragraph if you can.

See *Planning your essay* Ch 6.

Making it all flow

To make sure your essay is keeping on track and flowing well, with every paragraph contributing to answering the question and working towards your conclusion, do the following:

1 *At the end of each paragraph look back to the question. Can you see how the point you are making helps answer it? Would it help your reader to point this out? This is feeding back to the question.*
2 *Now think forward to the conclusion. How is the point you just discussed in the paragraph leading towards the conclusion? If it is an important finding, make a note at the end of your work to include it as part of your conclusion.*

If you cannot see how the paragraph feeds back to your question or forward to your conclusion then seriously consider removing it. It may be interesting but you could be going off the subject and using your precious word count on something that will not reward you with marks.

Signposting

This is really about leading your reader through your work so they can easily see where you are going.

You can do this by signposting in:

- the *introduction* – include a mini guide of what you are doing, why and how you will do this. You may have to rewrite this to make sure it actually matches what you did.
- *throughout the work*
  - at the start and end of paragraphs
  - within paragraphs to indicate a change of direction.
- the *conclusion* – what you did, found out, concluded and any implications.

See *Planning your essay* Chs 5 and 12.

Signal words help with signposting and may show:

> *order*: firstly, secondly …
> *adding points*: also, and …
> *examples*: for instance, such as …
> *other views*: although, yet, alternatively …
> *results*: so, consequently, it can be seen …

6 Appendices and checking

Appendices

Appendices can be useful if you need to provide extra evidence. If you include an appendix or appendices then you must refer to them in your text, otherwise why would your reader bother to look at them? Just put 'see appendix 1' in the text. If you have more than one appendix continue with the numbering, 2, 3 … etc. Make sure your appendices are in the order you use them in the body of your work.

The appendices should be placed after the reference section and page numbering should just continue on from the rest of the work.

Things you may include in the appendices are:

- raw data
- models
- transcripts
- interview questions

The appendix is NOT the place to hide your word count. Only information that may be of use to the reader should be included.

Checking

This is more than simply proofreading your work.

You should always check that:

- everything in the assessment criteria and learning outcomes is included
- there is a clear introduction

See *Planning your essay* Ch 11.

- there is a clear conclusion
- references are correctly included in the text and bibliography
- pages are numbered and line spacing guidelines followed
- any appendices are correctly numbered and in order.

Proofreading

- Read your essay aloud or use software or an app to do this for you, www.naturalreaders.com for instance. You will hear errors you can't see.
- Ask someone whose English you trust to read over it. It does not matter if it is not their subject. If you have written it well they will follow it. Ask them to point out where they don't understand as well as grammar/punctuation errors and review their suggestions.
- Leave it a few days if you can – otherwise you read what you think is there.
- Don't over worry about proofreading – you get most marks for your use of ideas and critical skills – not your spelling.

being academic

You could write a well-structured essay that flows perfectly but unless you write in an academic style, use reliable sources that are referenced properly and provide your reader with some critique of these sources you could still end up with poor marks. You may be amazed to know that the marks for the content or knowledge in your essay may be as low as 30%. Usually it is not WHAT you write but what you DO with this information that earns you the marks. That is, it is how how you argue it, reference it, draw your own conclusions, suggest implications and make any recommendations that really draws in the big marks. Look at your assessment criteria again – is it possible to work out how many marks are for critical analysis and making clear your own conclusions? It could be 40%, so make sure you go for these marks.

7 Academic style

This means writing formally and not being too chatty or descriptive in your writing. It also includes referencing correctly. Make an effort to do this as your department/institution requires as soon as you can.

See *Planning your essay* Ch 12.

You can help your academic style by being:

1 *formal* – don't write as you speak as you will end up sounding chatty. Imagine you are talking to your tutor, so no slang or phrases usually used in speech
2 *remote* – avoid 'I', 'you' or 'we', except in reflective writing
3 *concise* – try not to over-explain or over-describe. Avoid generalisations (*many researchers*) and vague terms (*thing, nice*)
4 *cautious* – say something 'may' happen (avoid saying it 'will' happen or you may have to prove it).

8 Using reliable sources

Your reading list is the starting point for your research. Your assessment criteria will usually require you to demonstrate you have used a 'range of reading/literature' in your work. You will get better marks if you go beyond the reading list and lecture material as this shows you to have independent research skills.

Your university will have access to databases with hundreds of academic journals. You can search these using keywords and limiters such as Boolean operators (AND, NOT, OR), year range, whether peer reviewed or not, to narrow your research area. It is worth learning how to do this – see your friendly librarian or just learn by experimenting with databases.

Journal articles are rated as they are usually more up to date and peer reviewed – that is, have been checked by other respected professionals in the field so are regarded as reliable. In fast-moving fields such as healthcare, science and business it is important to show you are aware of current ideas and trends.

It is worth finding out who your subject librarian is. They know their way around the best resources,

See *Planning your essay* Ch 9.

online and otherwise in your field, and will be keen to share this knowledge. They can also help with database searching and referencing.

9 Appraising the quality of the evidence

You should be aware research is not always good research and develop your skills in appraising the quality of the evidence. This is because you cannot make good judgements and conclusions from bad evidence. In some fields there are tools to help you (e.g. CASP and McMasters in healthcare) but you can start to do this for yourself by asking:

WHAT, WHO, WHY, WHEN, and HOW the research was written to test the reliability, objectivity and relevance of it. The 'my learning essentials' webpages from Manchester University library provide excellent interactive slides for this at: www.escholar. manchester.ac.uk/learning-objects/mle/evaluating-sources/.

- WHAT does it say, does it fit in with other evidence, if not why not?
- WHO is the author – a known name?
- WHY was it written – is there an agenda such as selling an idea or product? Is it biased?
- WHEN was it written? Is it current enough?
- HOW was it done – is the method good, does it prove what it set out to? A weak methodology leads to unreliable evidence.

Trust your own judgement. If you found it hard to follow or it did not convince you, then why not? Follow your instinct and track back to where it didn't make sense and analyse why this was. Maybe it made claims that were not supported in your view by the argument made and evidence presented. Do not be afraid to say so as long as you suggest why you think this. You are displaying criticality and this is what your tutors are looking for. You will be rewarded by improved grades.

10 Being critical

Once you have identified some sources you need to look across the research evidence you have collected and pull out the main points you need to discuss. When explaining your point keep your reader in mind and consider how much detail they really need to know. Try not to over-explain, we need you to get to what YOU think about the available evidence.

The critical stairway (Williams 2014) has steps to help you understand moving on from simply describing and understanding what you are reading. These are the critical steps of describing, analysing, comparing, synthesising, evaluating, applying and justifying information (Williams 2014, p14).

You may notice these steps reflect the language in your own assessment criteria, so they are worth explaining here.

Step 1	Describe	Understand and process information
Step 2	Analyse	Examine and see how parts 'fit' together
Step 3	Compare	Spot similarities and differences in ideas
Step 4	Synthesise	Pull together and connect sources
Step 5	Evaluate	Assess how good it is based on the evidence
Step 6	Apply	Use what you have gained from your critical evaluation
Step 7	Justify	Develop arguments, draw conclusions and implications from your critical thinking

Adapted with thanks from Williams (2014) Chs 3 and 14

See *Getting critical* Ch 3.

Getting stuck on Step 1 – describing – does not allow you to demonstrate clearly your critical skills and will cost you big marks.

11 Referencing

The concept

The concept of referencing – why we do it is really simple – is so YOUR reader knows:

1 exactly where in your work you used someone else's idea because you put a citation next to that information

AND

2 this leads them to easily find a full reference giving all the details (author, title, publisher etc.)

SO

3 they can go off and find exactly the same article, book, website or other source that you used.

Basically the rule is: if you had to 'read it to know it' then you must reference it. If in doubt reference it anyway. You won't lose marks for over-referencing but you certainly will for under-referencing.

All referencing systems have two aspects:

1 a small reference within the text (a citation)
2 a longer reference with all the details – usually at the end of your work.

Once you understand the concept of referencing, how to do it is a technicality. Do check which system you are supposed to be using and really get your head around it. This will gain you extra marks throughout your course and become second nature in the end. Well worth the effort!

See *Getting critical* Chs 3 and 14.
See *Referencing and understanding plagiarism*.

The most common referencing errors are:

- Not referencing someone else's work – ask yourself how you know it. If you read it, reference it. If in doubt, reference it.
- Not enough references – there should be references in every paragraph (excepting possibly the introduction and conclusion) and one is not enough. Aim for a minimum of three otherwise you cannot be seen to be using a 'range' of literature.
- Not including a page number when you quote. You can avoid this by rewording the original so it is clear you understand the idea. Then no page number is necessary but you **must** still reference it as it was not your original idea. If you must quote and cannot find a page number write 'no page' so at least your reader knows you knew you should include this.

See *Referencing and understanding plagiarism* and *Cite them right*.

4

improving for next time

After handing in your essay you will probably forget it until the results are released. But you can learn from the experience of writing every essay and continue developing your expertise. Analysing how you tackled the task this time and paying special attention to your feedback (especially the positive feedback you had which is so often ignored by students) will be time well spent.

12 Analyse how it went

Even a grade-A student can benefit from a little self-analysis: review what happened and see where you can improve. Here are some questions to help with this but as every student's experience is different, do try to think of your own.

- *What took most time?*
- *How could you refine/speed up this process?*
- *Is there an area that always lets you down?*
- *Did you miss out or include information not needed?*
- *Could your reader see a clear conclusion?*
- *Did you go off the point?*
- *Was your structure clear?*

Your questions?

- *...*
- *...*

Spend a little time trying to think how to overcome these challenges. This is metacognition or thinking about learning and will help improve your future performance.

13 Use feedback positively

Students' reactions to feedback can be very negative. A quick glance, maybe a sigh that referencing or critical analysis let you down again, and then it is put to one side. Resolve to change this now and use your feedback positively. It is a good idea to hunt out your last 2–3 assignments and analyse what went well and what didn't.

Go for the big mark makers to start with – usually accurate referencing and critical analysis.

If it is **referencing** that lets you down seek out any help you can: books, tutors, librarians, online help – most institutions have their own. If you cannot find other help try Oxford Brookes Upgrade Study Advice service's A–Z of Study Skills (select R for referencing and follow the links, starting with understanding the concept of referencing).

If it is **critical analysis** that lets you down the following is a useful technique to use your feedback to help you recognise where you have done this well:

Go through your feedback now, completely ignore any comments re punctuation or referencing for now. Focus on where you see any positive comments such as good point, good, a tick or well argued. Look back at what you wrote. What was it that the reader liked? Analyse this now.

It will usually be that you moved on from the original point somehow and showed what you made of it. Maybe you suggested how to use whatever it was in practice or pointed out why it could not be used. It

---

See *Referencing and understanding plagiarism* and *Cite them right.*

is likely, drawing on your reading, that you came up with something new, showing you could apply other people's ideas to your topic somehow.

Do this for several instances and try to see if a pattern emerges. This successful pattern is what the tutor was looking for. Now you have established what this is, try to replicate it in every paragraph you write.

Now look back and notice and learn how to correct any **referencing errors** (see p18).

References

Godwin J (2014). *Planning your essay* (2nd edition). Basingstoke: Palgrave Macmillan.

Manchester University Library (2014) *Finding the good stuff: evaluating your resources.* Available at: www.escholar.manchester.ac.uk/learning-objects/mle/evaluating-sources/ [Accessed: 16 March 2015].

Thomas G (2011). *Doing research.* Basingstoke: Palgrave Macmillan.

Williams K (2014). *Getting critical* (2nd edition). Basingstoke: Palgrave Macmillan.

See *Getting critical* and *Critical thinking skills* Ch 13.

Linked books in the *Palgrave Study Skills* and *Pocket Study Skills* series

Copus J (2009). *Brilliant writing tips for students*. Basingstoke: Palgrave Macmillan.

Cottrell S (2011). *Critical thinking skills* (2nd edition). Basingstoke: Palgrave Macmillan.

Godfrey J (2011). *Writing for university*. Basingstoke: Palgrave Macmillan.

Godwin J (2014). *Planning your essay* (2nd edition). Basingstoke: Palgrave Macmillan.

Greetham (2013). *How to write better essays* (3rd edition). Basingstoke: Palgrave Macmillan.

Pears R and Shields G (2013). *Cite them right* (9th edition). Basingstoke: Palgrave Macmillan.

Thomas G (2011). *Doing research*. Basingstoke: Palgrave Macmillan.

Williams K (2014). *Getting critical* (2nd edition). Basingstoke: Palgrave Macmillan.

Williams K and Carroll J (2009). *Referencing and understanding plagiarism*. Basingstoke: Palgrave Macmillan.

POCKET STUDY SKILLS
Jeanne Godfrey

WRITING FOR UNIVERSITY

POCKET STUDY SKILLS
Julia Copus

BRILLIANT WRITING TIPS FOR STUDENTS

POCKET STUDY SKILLS
Gary Thomas

DOING RESEARCH

POCKET STUDY SKILLS

READING & MAKING NOTES

Jeanne Godfrey

SECOND EDITION

POCKET STUDY SKILLS

STUDYING WITH DYSLEXIA

Janet Godwin

POCKET STUDY SKILLS

REFLECTIVE WRITING

Kate Williams, Mary Woollliams and Jane Spiro

POCKET STUDY SKILLS
Kate Williams & Jude Carroll

REFERENCING & UNDERSTANDING PLAGIARISM

PALGRAVE STUDY SKILLS

NINTH EDITION

CITE THEM RIGHT

THE ESSENTIAL REFERENCING GUIDE

RICHARD PEARS
GRAHAM SHIELDS

Notes

Notes

First published 2015 by
PALGRAVE

Palgrave in the UK is an imprint of Macmillan Publishers Limited, registered in England, company number 785998, of 4 Crinan Street, London, N1 9XW.

Palgrave Macmillan in the US is a division of St Martin's Press LLC, 175 Fifth Avenue, New York, NY 10010.

Palgrave is a global imprint of the above companies and is represented throughout the world.

Palgrave® and Macmillan® are registered trademarks in the United States, the United Kingdom, Europe and other countries.

ISBN: 978-1-137-55099-6   paperback

This book is printed on paper suitable for recycling and made from fully managed and sustained forest sources. Logging, pulping and manufacturing processes are expected to conform to the environmental regulations of the country of origin.

A catalogue record for this book is available from the British Library.

A catalog record for this book is available from the Library of Congress.